RELIANT

A 28 Day Journey to Draw Closer to God

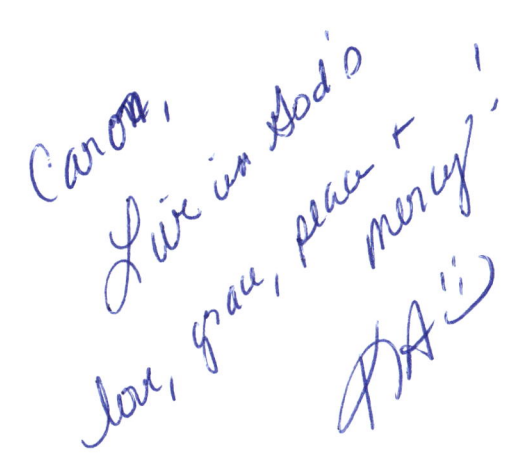

KELLYANN BOWMAN

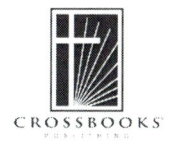

CrossBooks™
A Division of LifeWay
1663 Liberty Drive
Bloomington, IN 47403
www.crossbooks.com
Phone: 1-866-879-0502

© 2014 Kellyann Bowman. All rights reserved.

No part of this book may be reproduced, stored in a retrieval system, or transmitted by any means without the written permission of the author.

First published by CrossBooks 05/22/2014

ISBN: 978-1-4627-3700-0 (sc)
ISBN: 978-1-4627-3702-4 (hc)
ISBN: 978-1-4627-3701-7 (e)

Library of Congress Control Number: 2014907721

Printed in the United States of America.

This book is printed on acid-free paper.

Scripture quotations are from The Holy Bible, English Standard Version® (ESV®), copyright © 2001 by Crossway, a publishing ministry of Good News Publishers. Used by permission. All rights reserved.

Scripture quotations taken from the New American Standard Bible®, Copyright © 1960, 1962, 1963, 1968, 1971, 1972, 1973, 1975, 1977, 1995 by The Lockman Foundation. Used by permission. (www.Lockman.org)

Scriptures taken from the Holy Bible, New International Version®, NIV®. Copyright © 1973, 1978, 1984, 2011 by Biblica, Inc.™ Used by permission of Zondervan. All rights reserved worldwide. www.zondervan.com The "NIV" and "New International Version" are trademarks registered in the United States Patent and Trademark Office by Biblica, Inc.™ All rights reserved.

Scripture quotations taken from the Holy Bible, New Living Translation, copyright 1996, 2004. Used by permission of Tyndale House Publishers, Inc., Wheaton, Illinois 60189. All rights reserved.

Because of the dynamic nature of the Internet, any web addresses or links contained in this book may have changed since publication and may no longer be valid. The views expressed in this work are solely those of the author and do not necessarily reflect the views of the publisher, and the publisher hereby disclaims any responsibility for them.

Contents

Preface vii

Inextricably reliant 1
Crying out 7
Thinking upward 11
A prayer for God's will 15
Complete surrender 19
Love. Grace. Peace. Mercy. 23
The path 27
Balance 31
You are noticed 35
Being transformed 40
Bless the Lord 44
The image of God 48
Why ask, "Why?" 51
Who am I? 55
Hope 59
Stay close 63
Keeping guilt away 67
Ask, seek, knock 71
Needs are met 75

Strength in weakness 79
The power of thought 83
Living together 88
Acting instead of reacting 92
Earnestly seeking 96
Love's recordkeeping 100
Refuge 104
Going fishing 107
Insurmountable 111

Preface

I'm Kellyann and I'm so excited for you in your journey with Christ. My prayer is that you would use this devotional to draw closer to Jesus and be transformed by His grace. I accepted Jesus Christ as my Savior when I was 14 years old. I didn't start truly following Jesus as a devoted disciple until I was in my 40s. My life had reached a dark pit full of sadness, grief and anger and I was trying desperately to medicate through alcohol and ignoring God. I was angry at Him that He had allowed pain and grief and instead of turning *to* Him, I turned *away* from Him.

These devotions were first published on my blog and reflect my journey toward the goal of being inextricably reliant on my Savior. It is my prayer that by reading these entries and journaling your thoughts and prayers, you will also grow to be more reliant on God and allow Him complete control of your life. Total reliance on God is a transformational process. Be kind to yourself as you grow.

Many of these entries are chock full of Scripture passages (references are from the ESV, unless otherwise noted). A lot of God's work in my life has been as a result of time spent in His Word. Grab your Bible and see where the Lord takes you.

Each entry should take 3 to 5 minutes to read, plus time to reflect and write in the journal. My hope and prayer is that you would use these devotional readings to enter into a quiet time with our Redeemer at the beginning of each day. However, any time you can set aside to spend with Jesus will bless you tremendously and draw you closer to Him.

Inextricably reliant

"And when he got into the boat, his disciples followed him. And behold, there arose a great storm on the sea, so that the boat was being swamped by the waves; but he was asleep. And they went and woke him, saying, "Save us, Lord; we are perishing." And he said to them, "Why are you afraid, O you of little faith?" Then he rose and rebuked the winds and the sea, and there was a great calm. And the men marveled, saying, "What sort of man is this, that even the winds and sea obey him?" Matthew 8:23-27

"And a great windstorm arose, and the waves were breaking into the boat, so that the boat was already filling. But he was in the stern, asleep on the cushion. And they woke him and said to him, "Teacher, do you not care that we are perishing?" And he awoke and rebuked the wind and said to the sea, "Peace! Be still!" And the wind ceased, and there was a great calm. He said to them, "Why are you so afraid? Have you still no faith?" And they were filled with great fear and said to

> one another, "Who then is this, that even the wind and sea obey him?" Mark 4:37-41

> "And as they sailed he fell asleep. And a windstorm came down on the lake, and they were filling with water and were in danger. And they went and woke him, saying, "Master, Master, we are perishing!" And he awoke and rebuked the wind and the raging waves, and they ceased, and there was a calm. He said to them, "Where is your faith?" And they were afraid, and they marveled, saying to one another, "Who then is this, that he commands even winds and water, and they obey him?" Luke 8:23-25

I love the pictures in my head of these three accounts of Jesus' experience with His followers. Can't you just picture the disciples? Watching the storm hit, they frantically tried to keep afloat while the boat filled up with water, probably getting seasick from the dramatic tossing about, fearing they would die.

These fishermen knew what to do in a storm. Yet, this storm was wrecking them physically as well as emotionally. In the chaos of the situation, I imagine no one even thought to ask where Jesus was. I bet they figured He was somewhere on the boat, panicking like they were.

Can't you imagine one of the disciples, out of the corner of his eye, looks in Jesus' direction and realizes He's lying there — not moving. Maybe they thought He was dead! As this disciple gets closer, he would have realized that Jesus wasn't dead, but in fact, he's sleeping! Yes, sleeping!

Can you even imagine how you would feel? Take a moment to picture this scenario in your mind and feel the emotion behind this discovery.

If it were me, I would have been mad. I would have been thinking, Who is this guy Jesus, that we follow Him, and yet, He's asleep at our final hour! And what kind of a person can sleep through this storm, anyway? He must be ready to die to sleep through the torment here. I would be full of confusion and anger and sadness. Confusion over how He could sleep, anger about why He would sleep, and sadness that He *would* sleep. What would you be feeling?

When a storm hits in our lives, we see it and react through the lens of human nature and that causes fear. However, when a storm hits our lives, God sees it and reacts through the lens of eternity and that causes peace. Jesus wasn't being rude or trying to hurt the feelings of His followers by not responding how they expected. He was simply responding to the storm in light of eternity.

Jesus knew His life was in the hands of His Father and there was nothing to worry about! His faith was fully and inextricably reliant on God. In that, there was no *room* for fear. There was no need for fear. There was no purpose in fear. There was no fear.

Do you know what *inextricably* means? According to *dictionary.com*, it means being so entangled as to make escape impossible. Isn't it a great word!

I don't know about you, but I want my life to be so reliant on God that we're inextricably connected. I want to live in the knowledge that I can't escape His love, grace, peace and mercy. I want to be asleep during storms in my life — not because I don't want to feel them or deal with storms — but because my peace is so amazingly produced by God that I don't even register that a storm is taking place.

Maybe you are now saying to yourself, There's no way can I ever produce that kind of faith. I'm not able. I'm too nervous. I'm too anxious. (Maybe you are getting anxious just thinking about trying to *not* be anxious!)

Here's the awesome thing about God: You can't do it without Him, but He gives you everything you need. Jesus says in John 14:27 that He gave us a gift of His peace! If we are living our lives surrendered to Jesus, then, we have His peace. We can be asleep during the storms of our lives because He's given us the gift of His peace. Let that permeate your thoughts right now. Relax.

God doesn't put us through anything we can't handle with his help. He knows us better than we know ourselves. He knows our limitations and uses storms to grow our faith. Later, I'll share about some of the storms God has used to grow my faith.

Maybe you're in a storm right now. Maybe you are watching your ship fill up with water, and you are certain you are going to sink this time. Reach out to Jesus and ask Him to calm your storm. Remember you have His peace available to you.

Maybe you're in a calm place right now. Maybe you know the way you've reacted to storms in the past isn't peaceful. Start praying about how to react peacefully in the next storm now and build your faith through God's Word.

Maybe you've never considered giving your life to Jesus and feeling His peace. Turn to Him now. He'll be right there to give you His peace.

Journal Space

Crying out

"And we know that God causes all things to work together for good to those who love God, to those who are called according to His purpose." Romans 8:28 NASB

During my quiet time with God one morning, I found myself sobbing. This strong emotion overflowed out of two contributing factors: fear of God and love for God. It was really quite amazing to experience emotion from both ends of the spectrum in the same moment. On one hand, I felt overwhelmed with love for this God who has saved me from a life of utter despair. On the other hand, I felt fear over knowing that because He had control of my life, He could allow pain.

As I read more of the Bible, I am getting a better sense of who God is. Part of that character is violent to me, quite honestly. Lots of people died horribly within God's will.

Job lost his entire world in God's will. Jesus died a horrible death in God's will. The list could go on and on with examples from Scripture. The reality is God allows pain to enter our lives. Sometimes, He even brings pain into our lives for pruning.

The issue for us, as always, is how we respond. We can be fearful like I was feeling, or we can claim the power that He has given us. From His word, we are promised hope in Romans 8:28, *"And we know that God causes all things to work together for good to those who love God, to those who are called according to His purpose."* If I trust God and put my entire life in His hands, then the only response to the fear is repentance, and digging into the Word to draw closer to Him.

I want my response to challenges and trials to be, "God, this is your life, live it through me to bring glory to You."

It's more than a little frightening to be that open with God and give my life over to be used as He wills. I'm a control freak and am prone to anxiety and panic. Giving my life and my circumstances to God is a moment by moment endeavor. Some days are easy because the waves of life are small. Some days are harder because the waves of life are cresting my boat.

In the end, God is in charge of all things and He has my life in His very safe and capable hands, which means that I am never actually in danger. I may be in a situation where this physical existence is in jeopardy, but I don't have to be afraid because my eternal life is secure in His hands.

I'm certain that, for the rest of my life, this will be a moment to moment challenge. My heart desires to be like Paul and fully embrace Philippians 1:21, *"For to me to live is Christ, and to die is gain."* My natural response is much more like Peter, who after seeing Jesus transfigured into a glowing image and talking with Moses and Elijah said, *"… If You wish, I will make three tabernacles here …"* (Matthew

17:4 NASB) This verse is basically saying, Jesus, let's just stay here because it's all good right now.

God is frightening and yet, He is complete and utter love. If we can fully embrace that everything He does, He does out of love to bring glory to His name, then we can stop being afraid of our circumstances.

Nothing here on earth is bigger, stronger or in any way larger than our God and nothing catches Him off guard. If you fear God — if you are afraid of the bad things that could happen in your life, then pray and ask God to change that fear to peace. Remember that all things end up being for good when you are following God.

Journal Space

Thinking upward

"Set your minds on things above, not on earthly things."
Colossians 3:2 NIV

Our thoughts are one of the primary ways the enemy attacks us. He gets in our head and drops little bombs of unhappiness, discontent or fear. Then, we help detonate them by entertaining negative thoughts, instead of thinking upward, toward heaven.

My brain can go from a 0-to-60 velocity in 10 seconds on one thought. Before I know it, I'm thrown into a panic attack. Let me give you an example. A while back, I cracked a tooth. Now this cracked tooth went on for a long time with no pain or discomfort, so I figured it was no big deal. (Of course, the fact that I dislike going to the dentist aided in my ability to ignore this tooth.) One night, I got a screaming earache and toothache. From the time the ache began, until about 10 minutes later, I had moved from thinking "Oh, it's nothing" to "I'm going to get a brain infection from this dumb tooth and die!"

My heart was racing, my face was flushed. I was in full panic mode, because I let my thoughts go crazy. Have you ever done something like that? If my brain is set on earthly things, I never leave the house. My panic and fear gets all-consuming, because I know there is destruction around every single corner. I forget there is Someone much bigger on my side.

On the flip side, I am convinced that our thoughts are the primary way we stay close to God. When I wake up singing a song of praise in my head, it leads me to prayer and thanksgiving. When I face a challenge and immediately think of a verse or even the paraphrase of a verse, my thoughts are pointed upward. My spirit soars!

If you are reading this and thinking, "Kellyann, you don't know the script in my head. It's just too hard to think my way out of it!" I would agree with you. You can't do it on your strength, but you can change your thought habits and patterns with God's strength!

The second half of 2 Corinthians 10:5 says, *"We take captive every thought to make it obedient to Christ."(NIV)* When you feel your thoughts causing you to look at this world, instead of looking to heaven, take them captive. Stop them in their tracks at that moment, and pray, "God, stop these thoughts in my head." Then, replace them with praise. This is cumbersome at first, but over time it becomes a more instant response.

We all have chapters upon chapters of earthly thoughts in our head which are negative and destructive. It's time we rewrite those into words of beauty and love and set our thoughts on heaven, where we get to spend an eternity with our heavenly Father and loving Redeemer.

Set your mind on heaven. Speak out loud, "God loves me and His love is bigger than my negative thoughts." Write down Bible verses to carry with you. Read them when you feel your thoughts slipping to this world. Draw near to the God who is bigger than every negative thought you've ever had all rolled together.

Journal Space

A prayer for God's will

"Seek the Kingdom of God above all else, and live righteously, and He will give you everything you need."
Matthew 6:33 NLT

Seeking God's kingdom above our own desires seems like a lofty and unattainable goal. We so often use the excuse, "I'm only human," and assume it covers our sin and God will understand our shortcomings.

In the end, the only way to live a full life is to seek God at all times, as a practiced habit.

Sometimes, we get so far off the path God has planned for us that He has to put some serious roadblocks in our path to stop us from complete self-destruction. Thankfully, He did this for me, but it was a painful process. I had to give up habits I thought I needed to survive, love I thought was true and a heart that felt like it couldn't trust God. All through the process, God was right there — healing me, calling me, loving me and bringing me to the place where I could learn to trust Him.

Now that I am here, in the center of God's will for my life today, I never want to leave it. I have traded prayers of, "Please rescue me," for prayers of "Please keep me."

I've traded the question, "How can I numb this pain," for, "How can I help show them You will heal their pain if they'll just turn to You." It's a very different life I have now — one that is infinitely better than the one I had. There is no comparison.

I recently looked up many verses on God's will in my concordance and wrote them out in prayer form:

> Thank you, Lord, that you have caused my spirit to delight in doing your will and putting your law in my heart. (Psalm 40:8) May your will be done here on earth as it is in heaven, which is always. (Matthew 6:10) Lord, I know that is your will and desire. (Matthew 11:26) Thank you, Lord, that because I follow you and your will for my life, I am a sister to Jesus. (Matthew 12:50) Help me in my struggles to remember that Jesus struggled with your will too, yet He always had you and your will as His priority and only option. (Matthew 26:39) Thank you, Father, for my life. (John 1:13) Help me find nourishment in your Word always. (John 4:34) From that nourishment in your Word, keep me from conforming to this world and keep me renewed in my mind, so that I am always aware of your perfect will. (Romans 12:2) Father, keep my heart bound to you, and help me never seek to please anyone but you. (Ephesians 6:6) May my heart always be filled with knowing your will at all times.

> (Colossians 1:9) Lord, give me strength when doing your will is harder than I expect or imagine. (1 Peter 3:17) Remind me that this world ends, and that I will be with you forever. (1 John 2:17) Thank you, Lord, for hearing this prayer and for the confidence in my heart that you will answer me. (1 John 5:14). Amen.

Please put God in the center of your life. Seek to walk in the center of His will whatever the cost. He will meet you where you are, and He will bring you to places you never dreamed. You may be reading this thinking you don't need God in the center because your life is fine the way it is. Or you may be thinking you don't have the strength to turn to God. Or, worst of all, that God won't take you back because you've gone too far.

These are all complete and utter lies. If you will turn to God, you will find He will grab you and pull you in, before you even get fully turned around.

Journal Space

Complete surrender

"Abide in me, and I in you. As the branch cannot bear fruit by itself, unless it abides in the vine, neither can you, unless you abide in me." John 15:4

I used to think God would take what we give Him of our lives and be happy. I assumed he looked at my life and said, "Oh look, Kellyann has given me Sunday morning. Isn't that awesome!"

I am becoming more and more certain, however, that while God will take what we can give Him as a start, it is not where He wants us to stay. He wants us to get to the place of complete surrender. I use the term *want* very loosely because I actually think He demands that we give Him everything. Thankfully, He works with us to get us to that point.

Two passages in John 15 show me that God wants it all. John 15:4-11 is the description of the vine and its fruit. Verse 4 says, *"Abide in me, and I in you. As the branch cannot bear fruit by itself, unless it abides in the vine, neither can you, unless you abide in me."*

As long as the branch is connected to the vine, it has no choice but to do the will of the vine and produce fruit. It's what the branch was made to do!

A branch on the ground is nothing more than garbage. Jesus is our vine and if we want to live the life He has created us to live, we must be completely surrendered to Him to fulfill His calling in our lives. That calling is to produce fruit which brings glory to God. There is no choice. Just as a branch isn't going to one day decide on its own to jump off the vine, we must live so dependent on God that we will never choose to disconnect from Him.

In this same conversation, Jesus talks again about complete surrender. John 15:13-14 says, *"Greater love has no one than this, that someone lay down his life for his friends. You are my friends if you do what I command you."*

Jesus is defining *friend* as someone who is willing to give everything they have — to lay it all down — for another person. The flip side of Jesus giving His life for us is us giving our lives for Him.

Complete surrender. That's not just Sunday morning. It's all day, every day, 365 days a year, and 24 hours per day. If I am laying down my life for my friend, I am dying to anything I had planned for my life and giving Him complete control. Nothing about complete surrender is easy, but as you give your desires fully to Jesus, you experience a life that is exactly how God intended.

As you grow closer to Him, you may find that your dreams start coming true the closer you get to God. Your dreams start to change because they are conforming to the dreams and plans God has for your life. There may be pain as you are transformed into the person God created you to be, but the pain is temporary and is used to mold you and shape you.

In the end, God's plan for you is created out of this amazing love for you that, truly, we can't wrap our brains around. What you may think is best for your life may turn out to be only a garbage heap compared to what God wants to do with your life. Trust God. Give Him everything and seek to follow His plan for your life. There is no way you will be disappointed in the outcome when you abide in Christ. Ask God to show you how to abide in Him.

Journal Space

Love. Grace. Peace. Mercy.

Love. Grace. Peace. Mercy. Say these four words to yourself a few times: *Love. Grace. Peace. Mercy.* Let them soak in.

I live every day in light of these words. These four words float through my brain and my prayers so much that I've come to believe they are part of my DNA. I can't imagine my life without love, grace, peace or mercy. And not just those four aspects as random, but those four aspects as gifts from God.

I know God loves me because I see it in the people He has placed around me. When I get together with a group of women to pray on Tuesday mornings, I am encouraged by their faithfulness in prayer. I feel God's grace every time I make a mistake and He picks me up and says, "You are my daughter, keep going, I love you." I feel His peace wash over me like warm water whenever I have turmoil in my head and heart and I cry out for it to stop, Every day I get up knowing that my sins should have me in the darkest depths of life, but instead His mercy has saved me from the punishment I deserve.

What I am finding more fascinating about these four words is that they work together. Because God loves me, He extends grace, which allows me to feel His peace in my life and accept His gift of mercy. His grace is a gift of unmerited favor that I could never earn or deserve. Wow! The God of the universe, the Creator, the Supreme Being and God of all gods wants me to know He loves me, provides grace for me, bestows peace on me and gives mercy to me. Once I got a grip on that, what response could I give Him besides, "Thank you…take my life!"

Love: *Lamentations 3:22a, "The steadfast love of the Lord never ceases …"* Do you live as if you truly believe this? Do you get that this is saying that not only is God's love steadfast, or unwavering, it is forever! We have a God that loves us through anything and forever! Even if you don't fully understand and accept the grace, peace and mercy, get this point because it is critical and foundational for the others.

Grace: *John 1:16, "For from His fullness we have all received, grace upon grace."* We didn't just receive grace once, we receive it over and over and over and over. Grace upon grace! Heaps of grace. More grace than we can ever use up. Unmerited favor that is unending.

Peace: *John 14:27a, "Peace I leave with you; my peace I give to you."* The peace of Jesus. This is the man who fell asleep in the boat while a huge storm was raging and his disciples were completely freaked out and convinced they were going to die. I want this peace; don't you? This is peace that says to the storm, *you can stop now.*

Mercy: *Lamentations 3:22b, "His mercies never come to an end."* The next verse goes on to say that they are new every single morning we wake up. Just as we receive grace heaped upon itself, we also receive mercy that never stops. Once we accept Jesus as the Lord of our lives, we never receive the punishment we deserve. Instead, we receive unending mercy.

When you live fully in God's love, grace, peace and mercy, you live a life that is overflowing with joy. You are able to shine brightly for your Redeemer and show others a way to live in God's light. God's promises are always true so pray for Him to show you His love, grace, peace and mercy every day.

Journal Space

The path

> *"My sheep listen to my voice; I know them, and they follow me."* John 10:27 NIV

Change can be addicting. You may have heard of adrenalin junkies, but there are also change junkies and I am one of the latter. I love change because it's something new. There are no problems with new. Nothing has broken yet. I don't see other people's baggage and I haven't exposed my own. It's like a yard of snow that no one has walked on yet. It's fresh and untainted. Here's the problem with that: New snow doesn't stay new.

Because I enjoy change, I have a tendency to jump around. I've jumped from job to job, relationship to relationship, church to church. You get the picture.

As I grow in Christ, I no longer want to be a jumper. I want to be a follower. A follower is someone who walks a path already tread by the leader. A follower looks at the new terrain but doesn't choose the new terrain on their own.

As a follower, you might be able to see ahead, but you can't run ahead of the leader. The follower, by nature, is content to have limited influence, while putting complete trust in his or her leader.

Complete trust! Do you see the freedom in being a follower?!

Since I'm not responsible for choosing the direction, I can't ever get lost. I'm not responsible to review the terrain ahead and make sure I'm equipped. I get handed what I need and put it to use. I don't have to worry about the time because I don't set the pace. I get to enjoy the sights and sounds of the road I am traveling.

God is my leader which means that I have no fear, no worry, no needs. All I have to do is follow. He guides me exactly where I'm supposed to go. Do you feel the relief in that??

It's like floating on water.

Recently, I got off the path a little. I had to make a correction to get back on track. I was still following my Leader, but I was off in the bushes instead of on the right path.

In this situation, I made a commitment I shouldn't have made for a church ministry I shouldn't have jumped to. It was a new adventure for me and I was excited about the possibilities. I didn't think about it too much; I just jumped in feet first. When I realized what I'd done, I apologized, backed out and got back on track. I felt like the path I was on was too slow and boring. My desire to get further down the road distracted me and I jumped ahead of the leader.

I'm so thankful for God's voice and for the desire to seek God's voice. The peace I feel today after getting back on the path I'm supposed to be on is awesome. And God has used those around me to say, *Welcome back to the journey we are on.* Thank you, Lord!

I've traveled off the path so many times, and I'm finally in a place where I am asking God to keep me on His path. God doesn't call us to lives of constant change. Sometimes he calls us to routine, which can be boring. Listen to his voice and follow him. He'll never lead you astray.

Stay focused on the path. Seek help. Seek partnerships in prayer. Seek counseling. Seek God. He's the only true Leader for us. He's the only one who can keep us peaceful. He's the only One. If you've gotten off-track, ask Him to give you the strength to make the necessary changes, whatever they may be, to start walking with God again.

Journal Space

Balance

"The Jesus said to His disciples, "If anyone wishes to come after Me, he must deny himself, and take up his cross and follow Me." Matthew 16:24 NASB

Many people are seeking a life that has balance. When I think of the word balance, I think of something steady, that is weighted equally on all sides. There is a sense of harmony and peace when we feel like our boats aren't rocking any longer, but instead we are easing smoothly through the water. What does God say about balance?

My first thought was: Of course, God must want balance because balance feels like peace. However, if we truly want to seek God's answer related to balance for our lives, we have to look to his Word. I started to think about the people I've become acquainted with in the Bible — many lived their lives for God and seemed to be in the center of chaos.

In Luke 9:3, Jesus calls His disciples to a journey spreading the Good News, but taking nothing with them! He wanted them to completely trust Him with their needs and watch how He would care for them. That's not balance, it's surrender.

God calls us to be 100 percent devoted to Him and following His will. 100 percent devoted to God. There's no room for a half-hearted committment because He wants it all! He wants us to completely depend on Him to meet our needs. If by balance, I mean all sides are equal (my side and God's side), then that means I play a role in keeping things balanced. It suggests that I have a level of control, which is contrary to scripture.

In Matthew 16:24, as well as Mark 8:34 and Luke 9:23-24, Jesus tells us that in order to follow Him we have to deny ourselves and follow Him completely. Again, that's not balance, it's surrender.

Sometimes, we think: Lord, can't I just give you some free time that I have on Tuesday morning? The answer, of course, is that He'll take the time you have considered "free," but He wants *all* of your time. Not balance, but surrender. Everything we do should be to honor God — whether it's resting, working, helping others, or even having fun.

Jesus describes a conversation with a rich man who asks what he has to do in order to follow Jesus. (You can find the story in Matthew 19:16-30, Mark 10:17-31 and Luke 18:18-30.) After they establish together that this young man has been following the law, Jesus shatters his dreams by telling him that he must sell everything he has, give the money to the poor, and then follow Jesus. This young man's heart is broken and his choice is to walk away from Jesus because giving everything is just too much. Your circumstances may not be the same as the rich man's, but whatever your situation: God doesn't ask for balance, He asks for surrender.

My heart's desire is that we stop seeking balance and instead seek God and completely surrender to His will. It's a scary idea to give

Him everything, but He's always there to catch us and work out everything in our lives.

Make Him your primary relationship, and then everything else will fall into place. It likely will not happen overnight, but it will happen. You can surrender your life to Him. He will not forsake you. Instead, He will carry you to a deeper relationship. And as you travel through life and find that sometimes you stumble and take over your life again, pray for His help to give it back. He's always there with you.

Journal Space

You are noticed

And a great crowd followed him and thronged about him. And there was a woman who had had a discharge of blood for twelve years, and who had suffered much under many physicians, and had spent all that she had, and was no better but rather grew worse. She had heard the reports about Jesus and came up behind him in the crowd and touched his garment. For she said, "If I touch even his garments, I will be made well." And immediately the flow of blood dried up, and she felt in her body that she was healed of her disease. And Jesus, perceiving in himself that power had gone out from him, immediately turned about in the crowd and said, "Who touched my garments?" And his disciples said to him, "You see the crowd pressing around you, and yet you say, 'Who touched me?'" And he looked around to see who had done it. But the woman, knowing what had happened to her, came in fear and trembling and fell down before him and told him the whole truth. And he said to her, "Daughter, your faith has made you well; go in peace, and be healed of your disease."
Mark 5:24b-34

The woman in this passage had been bleeding for 12 years straight! That meant she was "unclean" for 12 years of her life. *Unclean.* In her world, that meant that not only was she herself considered dirty, but everything she sat on was also unclean — the bed she slept on, her blankets, her clothes and everything she touched.

Yet in the midst of her physical and emotion strain, she had hope. Her hope was based on her faith that Jesus could heal her. She clearly didn't want to bother Him or talk to Him. All she wanted to do was touch His clothes.

Do you get how much faith she had in such a small act? She didn't want Him to touch her, she didn't want Him to talk to her, she only wanted to be able to reach out and touch His clothes! How many times do we ask and sometimes even demand that Jesus do something big for us to help us have faith and yet this woman believed that if she just touched His clothes, He would heal her.

Now, take a look at the Healer, Jesus. Jesus is pressed in on all sides. It's likely many people were yelling at Him to get His attention. In the midst of this noisy, chaotic, mob-like situation, Jesus feels someone touch His garment in a way that is different from the others around.

He feels His healing power leave Him through His clothes! Now, in my mind, here's what I see happening next:

> This small woman walks up to Him. Her head is bent, with eyes cast down and hands covering her face. She has lived the last 12 years in such shame

that she doesn't know how to stand up straight anymore.

She drops to her knees, face down, while her body shakes with sobs and she tries with all her might to tell Him her story. I have no doubt she's apologizing along the way. The crowd has pushed back and created a circle of solitude between Jesus and this woman.

Jesus bends down and lifts up her face, with eyes that are pouring out love on this unloved woman. He tells her that she can have peace now because her faith in Him has healed her.

Jesus calls her out, sending the message that she is significant. She is noticed.

Oh man! I want to cry as I picture His face! Can you even imagine how she feels as she makes her way through this crowd and heads home, knowing that her life is now changed forever? In the midst of chaos and people, Jesus noticed this woman's faith, met her need and healed her.

Jesus is waiting to do that same thing for you and for me. We move through the crowds in our lives. We hold fast to our faith that He is our Healer. We reach out to "touch His garments." Then, He notices us and he heals us.

Does this mean He always heals us *physically*? No. Not always. But He will always change our lives in a major way, and He will always bring about some type of healing, even if it isn't quite what we expect. For this woman, the bigger outcome is proof that her faith was placed in the right person, Jesus.

Place your faith in Him. Reach out at all costs. Be determined to "touch His garment." Get close to him. And, He will notice you and will meet you in your need. Even the ones you aren't aware of.

Journal Space

Being transformed

"And do not be conformed to this world, but be transformed by the renewing of your mind, so that you may prove what the will of God is, that which is good and acceptable and perfect." Romans 12:2 NASB

Transformation is a process; and a process implies work. Work is most often challenging. God is the driving force behind our transformation and the Spirit that enables us to make any changes at all, but there is still work on our end and it is sometimes painful. However, the outcome allows us to shine brightly for Jesus.

Instead of being transformed, sometimes I'd like the option of being *transferred*. Transferred to a personality where my ego doesn't get bruised. Transferred to a place where it isn't a chore to think first, and speak later. Transferred to a state where I don't feel second best. Transferred to a secure foundation where I don't battle with feeling replaceable.

Here is my dream scenario: I became a Christian, and I was instantly transferred to being a new person, someone who is transformed! No process to work through. No challenges of rewriting old habits. No need to shut my mouth. Just boom! In a flash … I could be transformed! (Someone needs to design a "Christian Transformer" doll that is all mangled at first, but with a few quick turns, it becomes beautiful!)

Alas, the above description is not God's plan for us. Transformation, by definition, is a process. Process, by definition, is a series of steps directed toward an end result. Therefore, the Christian life, as we are being transformed, is the process of moving toward heaven and perfection.

We won't ever reach a place while on earth that we can say, "I am fully and utterly transformed!" We will say that one day, the day we stand before the Father, next to the Son, and he says, "… *Well done, good and faithful servant! …*" (Matthew 25:23 NIV) I hope to hear, "Come here and give me a hug!"

Because it is a process that won't end until we're in heaven, we must follow the words of Paul in Philippians 3:14, *"I press on toward the goal to win the prize for which God has called me heavenward in Christ Jesus." (NIV)*

The year 2011 was a big year for me. I gave up unhealthy habits and unhealthy relationships to live my life for God. I gave every inch of my life over, and God healed me in ways I never imagined possible. He filled my cup to overflowing, and then some. I am forever thankful for this grace.

However, I got a little cocky with my relationship with God and started 2013 feeling like this was the year to keep digging deeper, but thought that I didn't really have much to work on. The delusion lasted exactly nine days. Then, I was flooded with all kinds of things God wants to work on.

At first, I was a bit overwhelmed. In my natural pattern, I started trying to think of how *I* was going to transform myself. Did you catch that? *I* was trying to figure out how *I* was going to transform. My thinking was so off the mark, that it's laughable. By the end of the day my prayer was, "God continue to transform me, please. Don't let me be a barrier. Only through Your power will I transform into the daughter You want me to be and bring You all the glory."

Every day I am on this earth, I will be transforming. God will transform my words from those which tear down others critically, to words which build up others supportively. He will transform my ego from feeling bruised and hurt by things that should not be personal, to an ego that is continually striving to die to itself so that Christ may live through me. He will transform my heart from feeling like I can be easily replaced because I'm not that important, to realizing that I am loved for who I am, and that I was created by the God of universe to be right where I am.

Journal Space

Bless the Lord

"Bless the Lord, O my soul, and all that is within me, bless His holy name!" Psalm 103:1

I have this extremely bad tendency when I'm down to go it alone, by beating myself up or listening to Satan's lies. Instead of blessing the Lord with thankfulness for all He has done for me, I go into this mode of inward focus. Maybe you've experienced it?

One day, while I was caught up in this vortex of inward negativity, I felt prompted to ask a friend to pray for me. Almost instantly, God rained down so much love on me that my tears of sadness and pain immediately turned to tears of joy! In a moment, God was speaking to me from many different sides and telling me how much He loves me. Because I think God has a sense of humor, I'm sure each "I love you" was followed by "duh."

I had been praying all morning on my own, but I needed a reminder of truth from my community. Instead of turning to God's word or close friends, I was firing off "help me" prayers. It was as if I was standing in the mud with my hands down at my sides sinking further and further while screaming, "HELP ME!" Yet, I wasn't reaching for the branches hanging above my head. I wasn't striving to get out of the mud that would eventually draw me under.

The branches — God's word and the people He has placed in my life — are always available and I need to be willing to reach out. I'm a slow learner, but I'm learning to see and hear God at work.

As soon as I lifted my hands that day to reach for my friend, I stopped sinking. As soon as I reached out to my friend to pray for me, I stopped sinking. As soon as I opened God's word, He started lifting me. By the time the day ended, I had shared time with another believer at work and spent time in the evening talking about how much God means to me.

I started the day with tears of frustration, sadness and pain. I ended the day with tears of joy while telling of the remarkable love of God.

In thankfulness, I read Psalm 103 and made it a prayer. Will you join me in this prayer?

> *Bless You Lord, O my soul, and every part of me. Bless Your holy name. Bless You Lord, O my soul, don't let me forget all that You have done and continue to do and will do in the future for me. Thank you for forgiving all my sins and making me clean. Thank you for saving me from hell both here on earth and after I'm dead. Thank you for filling my life with Your amazing love and mercy that never goes away. Thank you for giving me good things and renewing my spirit. Thank you for being righteous and saving me from oppression. Thank you for speaking to us for all these thousands of years.*

Thank you for being merciful and gracious. Thank you for not reacting in anger but showing me your amazing love. Thank you for covering your anger toward my sin with the righteousness of Christ. Thank you that you don't do to me what I deserve or hold my sin against me. Thank you that I can't reach heaven in this body and that I can't go outside Your love for me. Thank you for taking my sins so far from me that I can never get to them again. Thank you for a compassionate earthly father who shows me that though he loves me so much. Yet, You love me even more. Thank you for knowing me, Kellyann, and all my flaws and the fact that I am really just dust. Thank you that though my days are like grass and flowers that are so temporary, Your love goes forever without end. Thank you that everything is under Your rule in heaven. Bless You Lord, O my soul, thank you for all the heavenly beings who do Your will, who listen to You and minister for You. Bless You Lord, and all you do for me and that there is no where I can go that You aren't in control. Bless You Lord, O my soul.

Journal Space

The image of God

"So God created man in his own image, in the image of God he created him; male and female he created them."
Genesis 1:27

Have you ever really thought about this verse and what it means? Which part of me is the "image of God"? As I sat on a street bench one day, waiting for my bus and watching people go by, I was struck with a thought: We are so different from each other. No two of us are alike. Grey hair, brown hair, pink hair, no hair. Short or tall, fat or skinny. Laughing or sad, smiling or crying. Tattooed and pierced or conservatively dressed. I saw so many differences I couldn't keep track! It is overwhelming to think that despite all of the variety, we are all made in the image of God.

I started to ponder which part of me — and you — is God's image, trying to drill down to the level of the common denominator. In the end, I decided that our souls are the only true commonality. Through our faces and our body language, we communicate the current state of our soul. If we've had a bad day, we may look sad or stressed. If we've had a good day, we may look happy and smiley.

The question I had to ask myself was: Regardless of the kind of day I've had, do I convey God's love because I am made in His image? Does my face cause people to ask themselves why I look so relaxed, happy or loved? Am I making eye contact with people? Am I smiling through our interaction, even if it only lasts for two-seconds, as we pass each other on the street? Am I looking for an opportunity to reach out and share God's love with someone through a smile, a "Hello," or perhaps, a hand to help someone step off the curb?

The world is full of people who don't know the love, grace, peace and mercy of God. I need to be open to sharing Him. I need to remember that I am made in the image of the God of the universe. This means that I am actively seeking to love people as He loved me.

He loves me, and each person I encounter. He loves us so much that He sent His only Son to die for our sins, so we could have a relationship. That's news worth sharing and sharing loudly!

As you move through your days, try to remember that you are made in God's image and that His image is full of love for all people. Let me say that again, God's love is for all people, and you are made in the image of God — and so is everyone else. Show each other love, grace, peace and mercy.

Journal Space

Why ask, "Why?"

"The Lord directs our steps, so why try to understand everything along the way?" Proverbs 20:24 NLT

Why? Though an important question in some situations, it is a frustrating question when it comes to the struggles we face in life. Why emotional pain? Why physical pain? Why can't I get a better job? Why can't I find a job? Why is my spouse angry? Why don't my children listen? Why, if you are a loving God, did you allow this circumstance into my life?

Let's take a quick look at the character Job from the Bible. When he sat on a trash heap, scraping at his skin, he didn't understand why God had taken everything away from him. Do you think if God had answered his why question, it would have helped his pain? I don't. Asking why doesn't change the situation or take away the pain, it just adds more information to process, and that's not always helpful.

Because God is our Father, like any parent, He's got more information than we do and He understands the direction we are headed. His answer, most of the time, to our question *why* is, "Because I said so, and I'm your Father, and I know what's best."

My mom died suddenly and unexpectedly. I was talking to her on a Wednesday evening around 5:30 p.m., and an hour or so later, she was in an ambulance and I never saw her again. She had an aneurysm that her brain just couldn't recover from, and so, she went on to be with God.

My mother and I didn't have a typical mother-daughter relationship. My mother was the center of my world, the glue that held everything together. I worked to support her and my daughter, and she did everything else. That's no exaggeration.

When my mother died, I didn't know where we banked or how to pay the bills. I didn't know how to use the brand new washing machine. My mother did it all. Losing her was a blow I almost didn't survive. And how many times do you think I shook my fist at heaven, so angry at God I could barely keep my sanity in check, screaming "WHY!"? (Too many times to count.)

In the midst of my pain, I got no response. God was directing my path in a way I was not interested in following at first. But the truth that I understood later was the reason for the pain was to get me back on the path He had for me.

See, I had wandered so far away that God was just a shadow in my life, not the central figure He should be. I didn't need Him because I had my Mom! I knew enough about God to believe in what Jesus had done for my sins, but I didn't want to have a true relationship with God. What on earth could He do for me that my mom wasn't already doing?

It took me three and a half long and painful years of drinking, hurting, finding myself in places I shouldn't be, and spending time with people I shouldn't, to finally get an answer.

God knew my mom was His daughter and that she was going to a better place with Him. He also knew that I would never figure out how much I needed Him with her here and that she could help me more than she ever had here on earth by being in Heaven with Him. So, He took her.

Even though my initial reaction was to run even farther away, the running was actually towards Him.

My rebellion got me to the place of sitting in a hospital emergency room having an anxiety attack that I thought was a heart attack only to find out later that my heart physically started hardening. It was a medical condition. It was at this point that I finally gave up. I gave up the anger. I gave up running. I gave up friends and habits that were taking me in the wrong direction. I cried out, "SAVE ME!" and God said, "Here I am."

God directs your path — not you. He has ultimate control. He may let you wander, but He will never let you go. The next time you are faced with a challenge and want to ask "Why," try thanking God for the growth opportunity instead. Then, ask Him what He is trying to teach you.

Journal Space

Who am I?

> *"But you are a chosen race, a royal priesthood, a holy nation, a people for his own possession, that you may proclaim the excellencies of him who called you out of darkness into his marvelous light. Once you were not a people, but now you are God's people; once you had not received mercy, but now you have received mercy."*
> 1 Peter 2:9-10

Let me bring you into my inner circle for a moment and share a secret: I don't think very well of myself sometimes and this hinders my ability to proclaim God. I am haunted by the feeling of being a complete and utter failure in life and I don't easily see the positive impact I may have on people. I see the good in other people all the time, but I don't extend that vision and grace to the person I see staring back in the mirror. It's something I've been praying about fervently and something God is miraculously answering!

In 1 Peter chapter 2, my favorite disciple is telling us to understand and embrace who we are now that we are believers of Jesus. In the first few verses, he's telling us to put away the negative attributes of self and seek after a life that is nourished by "spiritual milk," or God's

Word, so that we grow in our faith. He calls believers a "living stone" and "chosen and precious." That's amazing!

Peter is telling us all that we are chosen and precious. God chose us and we are precious! Say it like this right now, *God chose me and I am precious.*

Do I sin? Yes. Do I struggle against my human nature? Yes. Am I forgiven? Yes. Am I chosen and precious? Yes! Yes! *Yes!*

In verses 9-10, Peter further defines who we are as believers. A royal Priesthood. A holy Nation. God's possession. A people. Receivers of mercy. If God sees me as all of these things, and He knows every single fiber of my being, how can I ever feel that I am anything but blessed and lovely in His sight?

To think I am a failure and not worth anything flies in the face of what God is telling me in His Word. My response is also called out by Peter. I should be able to *"proclaim the excellencies of him who called you out of darkness into his marvelous light."*

If I'm only looking inward at my flaws and my past then it's like taking a flashlight and putting it against my stomach. It does no good whatsoever because the light is blocked completely. Only when I accept my calling to a royal priesthood, a holy nation, a possession of God, and a receiver of mercy can I turn the flashlight around and shine His light on the people around me who are still in the darkness.

Don't let your past take away the light that God has called you to be. Move the flashlight away from pointing inward. Instead, point it outward so others can see the remarkable work God is doing in your life and be drawn to His light. When it is difficult to see the changes God is making in your heart, ask him to show you. And, ask a friend.

Journal Space

Hope

> *"The steadfast love of the Lord never ceases; His mercies never come to an end; they are new every morning; great is Your faithfulness. 'The Lord is my portion' says my soul, 'therefore I will hope in Him.'"* Lamentation 3:22-24

Life is sometimes challenging and can wear us down. It is hard to consistently feel the truth that God's love never ends, that He offers new mercy every morning or that He is faithful. It is in those times when we need to seek out His Word and the promises He has given us about His heart for us.

"The steadfast love of the Lord never ceases ..." God's love is solid no matter what is happening because it is steadfast. It never changes. It never fluctuates with your mood. It is never far away. It is always directed toward you and with you — no matter what is happening in your life. You can't escape it, and you can't do anything to earn it.

Isn't that awesome? I know it's hard to believe for some of us because we feel like we've gone too far and God can't love us anymore. Trust me, friend, that thought is a lie you don't want to believe because it can rob you of everything God has for you. Trust God that His love is steadfast and never ceases.

"His mercies never come to an end; they are new every morning …" There is no point at which God will say, "Sorry, I have no more mercy for you, you used it all up!" His mercy for you is not only unending, it's new every morning! So, when you feel like God can't forgive you anymore because you've done too much wrong, speak this verse to yourself and replace the lie that Satan is feeding you. God can and will forgive you and pour His amazing mercy on you at any point if you repent with a sincere heart.

"Great is Your faithfulness." His great faithfulness is shown as true through the promise that His mercies never end and are renewed every single morning.

"The Lord is my portion" says my soul, "therefore I will hope in Him." All you need is God. His love and mercy are all you need to get through every single moment of every single day of your life. Does that mean every day is wine and roses? No. Does that mean that you won't stumble and fall? No. It means that at every moment of your life, you have a choice to make: Choose God's steadfast love and unending mercy or yourself.

For me, there is no option. It's God every time.

God has so much He wants to do in your life, so don't be a barrier to His work in your life. Go to God, confess whatever you need to confess, ask for help. Then, accept His amazing love, grace, peace and mercy. He's just waiting for you to turn around. Once He sees you starting to move, He'll swoop in and save you. He won't always stop the natural course of events. He doesn't say you'll never have pain, but He does say that His love and mercy are there for you at any time or situation. Grab hold of that truth and never let it go.

Journal Space

Stay close

"O Israel, stay away from idols! I am the one who answers your prayers and cares for you. I am like a tree that is always green; all your fruit comes from me."
Hosea 14:8 NLT

Have you ever been in a relationship with someone that starts off as amazing, and then, you find that as time passes, you aren't as close as you used to be? There were things about this other person that you thought would keep you linked forever and allow nothing between you, but now these same things seem to bug you.

Maybe you would stay up for hours, talking about nothing and everything, but now you're indifferent to the sound of his or her voice. What happened?

Relationships are work. Staying close to someone requires a dedication that doesn't last unless you focus your attention on maintaining the relationship. That way, when you sense distance of any kind, you can fix its cause.

Our relationship with God is no different except for one thing … God never moves away.

When we first become a Christian or rededicate our lives, there is a level of emotion similar to being in love. God has rescued us from something or worked a miracle that causes us to be grateful, and we devour everything about Him.

Then, normal life creeps in, and we are still thankful for all God has done, but we get less thankful for what God is doing. We move from present tense to past tense with God, and we stop holding His hand. And in doing that, we put an idol in God's place and forget that He answers our prayers and cares for us.

The situation God has released us from, or the health scare that God healed, is now a distant memory. We're doing fine now, so we move a step or two out of sync with Him. We start to believe the lie that says we can do life just fine on our own. We don't always say it out loud, but we think, "Thanks, Mr. God, I'll let you know when I need you. I'll be sure to call now and then."

God's reply is, "Stay close. I am your tree of life."

Confession time … I have done this. I have started to move away from God. I had a life-changing moment with God. For the following eight months, I was so dedicated to spending hours in the Word and prayer that it was all-consuming. I used to joke that I was in spiritual rehab because God was doing a lot of healing and a lot of work.

As time went by, I started to feel like I could do a little more on my own and didn't need to rely on God as much. I didn't wake up at 4 o'clock in the morning anymore to read the bible and pray for 90 minutes. Instead, I woke up at 5:15 in the morning and spent 15 minutes starting my day with God. I didn't pray over my friends and family as much, I shot up a one sentence prayer, "Bless everyone in my life."

I didn't stay close.

Now, here's the wonderful truth about God: Wait for it … God never moves. *God never moves*!

When we start to feel distance between us and God, it's our fault, not God's. The minute that distance is recognized, you can always turn back because God never moves — whether it's been growing for five minutes, five days, five years or five decades. He is always right there by your side. He is always going ahead of you. While it may feel like He is far away, the truth is you can't trust your feelings, you must trust your faith in His Word which says He never leaves you and never forsakes you.

My encouragement for you today is to turn back to God and get close. It may not happen overnight, but it will happen if you seek God first and work to remove any barriers. This isn't an easy process necessarily, but it is worthwhile.

Journal Space

Keeping guilt away

"I was blameless before him, and I kept myself from my guilt." Psalm 18:23

Guilt is a hard habit to break. I believe that once I confess a sin and repent from it, I am forgiven. But letting go of the haunting reminder of my mistakes is still challenging.

Guilt is like the annoying fruit fly that hangs around long after the banana has been thrown away. Even though you can't always see it, it's still there. Just when you think it's gone, it flies in front of your face.

I have purposed to find verses that support the truth that I'm a new creation in Christ … my past is behind me and has no place in my present or my future. As I was reading through Psalm 18, I came across an absolute gem. Psalm 18:23 says, *"I was blameless before him, and I kept myself from my guilt."*

This verse seems to imply that if I can keep myself from my guilt, then I can also keep myself *in* my guilt. When thoughts creep into my head that make me rehash my mistakes and my sins, I need to shift my thoughts.

I need to recall verses like Philippians 3:13-14, *"Brothers and sisters, I do not consider myself yet to have taken hold of it. But one thing I do: Forgetting what is behind and straining toward what is ahead, I press on toward the goal to win the prize for which God has called me heavenward in Christ Jesus."* (NIV)

When I sit in the muck and mire of my past, I stop focusing on the life God has planned for me because I get caught up in negative thoughts that cause me to doubt God's plan for my life.

The first step is to retrain my mind to stay focused on the goal and not rehash the past. Then, the next step is to keep myself from doing the things that make me feel guilty in the first place.

It isn't possible to not sin. I'm going to do it every day. However, when I follow closely to God, I'm less likely to make the big mistakes that cause me pain and bring on heavy guilt. I must remember that though I may face temptation, God has already provided an escape for me.

1 Corinthians 10:13 says, *"No temptation has overtaken you except what is common to mankind. And God is faithful; he will not let you be tempted beyond what you can bear. But when you are tempted, he will also provide a way out so that you can endure it."* (NIV) How awesome is that? I belong to a God who not only understands my temptations, but also provides an escape route.

My prayer now is that I seek forgiveness immediately and make sure my relationship with God is restored. God never throws our past back at us. So, whenever guilty feelings start to come, I pray for

God's peace and remind myself of the promise of forgiveness from His word.

If you are feeling guilty about something, pray and ask God to show you if you need to repent and seek forgiveness. If your relationship with God is intact, know that the enemy is the one reminding you of your past mistakes and not your Heavenly Father. Pray and read the Bible in order to overcome guilty thoughts and keep yourself close to God, living in the overflow of His amazing forgiveness.

Journal Space

Ask, seek, knock

> *"Ask, and it will be given to you; seek, and you will find; knock, and it will be opened to you. For everyone who asks receives, and the one who seeks finds, and to the one who knocks it will be opened. Or which one of you, if his son asks him for bread, will give him a stone? Or if he asks for a fish, will give him a serpent? If you then, who are evil, know how to give good gifts to your children, how much more will your Father who is in heaven give good things to those who ask Him!"*
> *Matthew 7:7-11*

It had been a very rainy week. I live in the Seattle area, so I don't usually get upset by the rain, but this week was different. I was moving over the weekend, and I was bummed by the rain. I had prepared by ordering a rental truck, so that our furniture and boxes wouldn't get too wet.

I asked God to please allow for a small window of dry hours when my friends were coming to help. The day before the move I found out the rental truck wasn't available at the time I reserved. I had a moment of panic! People were scheduled and I had already signed my lease, so *not* moving wasn't an option. I wasn't sure what to do.

Very quickly, I turned my panic into prayer and asked God to help me. I knew that the move was in His plan for us, so I knew He was in the midst of this situation. My panic turned to peace because I knew that God would work everything out for my good and His glory.

The next day, all my friends showed up and we loaded a trailer, a couple of trucks and many cars. Guess what?

We didn't need the rental truck after all! All of our things fit in all the vehicles we had and we didn't even need to make a second trip!

You know what else didn't happen that day? Rain. God took a stormy, nasty, rainy week and gave me a day of dry weather. My belongings didn't get drenched and neither did my friends.

You know how else God provided? We had already planned a vacation for the next week, but I couldn't really afford the rental truck and vacation. I believed that God wanted us to go on the trip and so I knew He would provide the spending money needed. By not having the rental truck, I had the extra spending money we needed for our trip. God is good, all the time!

How many times in life do we forget to ask God to help us? We don't seek Him in the situation and we don't knock at the throne of the Father and share our need.

Yes, God knows everything and sees our needs, but the asking is important. The asking, the seeking and the knocking all allow us to put down our own strength and acknowledge that we can't get through a situation without Him. We need Him to meet our needs.

I could have chosen to get stressed out about the rain and the missing rental truck. Instead, I gave my situation to my Father in heaven who loves me more than anyone else. By giving my stresses and concerns to God, He is able to show His steadfast love and mercy to me, and ultimately, I am able to praise Him and give Him glory.

I can't tell the story of my moving without sharing how good God is and how faithful He was to meet my every need.

Ask. *Seek*. And, *knock*. Remember that you are asking your Father in heaven — the God of the universe — and He is just waiting for you to accept His gifts of love, grace, peace and mercy. God cares about your rainy days and your lack of a rental truck because He cares for you.

Journal Space

Needs are met

"And my God will supply every need of yours according to His riches in glory in Christ Jesus." Philippians 4:19

"God is good!" I wrote this in my journal one morning, when my heart was heavy. I had recently moved to a place that made my commute to work much longer. I was certain the move was God's will for our lives, my daughter and me, but the loss of two hours a day was very challenging for me.

My mornings were no longer leisurely and I had less time to get stuff done around my house. I went from driving to taking the bus, which added the extra pressure of needing to leave the house on time or get stuck taking a later bus and getting to work later.

On top of this, my daughter was having her own struggles with this loss of time together. I knew God would meet our needs, but I was struggling to see how.

My journal entry started off with "Thank you," and "Help me, please." My heart's greatest desire is to be close to God — so close that He is my all-in-all and my every thought.

However, I'm human (as much as I dislike that) and I don't stay this close to him at all times. I let life interfere sometimes. And, that's what I was doing this morning.

I knew God had carried me so far already, and He wasn't going to drop me now. I wanted to look up the verse in Philippians that says basically that He's begun a good work in me and He's able to bring that good work to its natural end.

In my head, I thought the verse reference was Philippians 4:19. When I opened up my bible and read that Scripture, I literally burst into sobbing tears at how lovingly and tenderly God met me and answered my need.

> **"And my God will supply every need of yours according to His riches in glory in Christ Jesus." Philippians 4:19**

Wow! I thought I needed to hear one thing from God, but He addressed the even bigger issue by coming right to where I was and speaking directly to my heart.

I didn't even see the need I had, but He did, and He met that need. In fact, he reminded me that he'll meet *all* my needs.

I don't have a need He can't meet! And not only that, but I don't have a need He won't meet! The challenge for me, and you, is to be watching for how He is meeting a need because it isn't always how we expect. Sometimes He changes us so the need changes and sometimes He changes the need so that we change.

God is good. He is with you every step of the way. So don't worry, don't stress. And, don't take matters into your own hands … Trust Him.

He says He'll meet your needs and He will. Be patient and watch what He'll do. It may not be today and it may not be tomorrow, but He will meet your need in His perfect time.

Journal Space

Strength in weakness

> *"Therefore, in order to keep me from becoming conceited, I was given a thorn in my flesh, a messenger of Satan, to torment me. Three times I pleaded with the Lord to take it away from me. But he said to me, 'My grace is sufficient for you, for my power is made perfect in weakness.' Therefore I will boast all the more gladly about my weaknesses, so that Christ's power may rest on me." 2 Corinthians 12:7b-9 NIV*

We all have challenges in life. Sometimes those challenges come back over and over again, like a "thorn in my flesh." I think of fear as my thorn in the flesh. Fear has kept me from going to meetings above the fifth floor in a building because of elevators. Fear has kept me from nice vacations because of flying. Fear has kept me in my home because of panic attacks. Fear kept me from being with my mom the last few days of her life because of the unknown.

I have let fear dominate, and in many situations, completely control my life. I have asked God to take away the fear completely more times than I can count, but it never goes away. It's the very quiet voice in the corner of my mind saying, "You can't do this. Remember, you're afraid." And every time I give in to that fear — the defeated feeling that I can't do something — I turn my focus from God and put it on myself.

I recently had to fly for a business trip. Here are the main fears I have had to wrestle with: the physical act of flying, riding the elevator in the hotel and leaving my daughter in the care of other people.In the past, I would simply have made up an excuse, so I wouldn't have to deal with the fear. That works in getting me out of the situation, but it leaves me to deal with the disappointment in myself.

When I gave my entire life and heart to Christ, I declared to myself and everyone around me that Christ was my all-in-all. Getting rid of baggage that needed to go was challenging, but relatively it was easy, because I was on the ground and not facing one of my bigger fears. With flying, I have to face multiple fears. Through processing my fear and following through on the business trip, my faith was tested.

I wasn't testing God. God's able to do immeasurably more than my small mind can ask or even imagine (Ephesians 3:20). God was testing my faith!

Am I able to trust God not only with my daily life in my hometown, but also in the air, in the elevator and 2000 miles away from my daughter? Am I able to trust that everything and anything that happens is for my good and will bring glory to God? Am I able to trust that God's plan really is the best plan for my life and really does mean hope and prosperity? Yes. Yes. Yes!

I'm not asking God to take away the fear, I'm asking God to come with me in all situations and remind me that His grace is sufficient no matter what happens (2 Corinthians 12:7-9). I'm asking Him to show me that He will supply all my needs (Philippians 4:19). I'm asking Him to remind me that He's going with me and all I need to do is follow (Deuteronomy 31:6). I'm asking Him to remind me that His plan is good (Jeremiah 29:11).

Find scripture to help you in challenging times. If you saw my Bible, you would see lots of tabs sticking out of it, marking verses that have helped me keep faith in God. I am reliant on God's word to get me through every single day. It's truly like oxygen for me, not to sound cliché.

Without God's word I'm lost. I can't hear from Him; I can't feel His peace and comfort when the fear creeps in. I encourage you to spend time in the Word. Let it become another part of your being, like your hands, feet or any other part of you needed to get you from one point to the next.

Journal Space

The power of thought

> *"… And take every thought captive to obey Christ …"*
> *2 Corinthians 10:5b*

Our thoughts shape the way we are going to handle the day. I woke up one morning from a dream that had already started my thoughts down a destructive path. It was a place I had gone many times.

My dream involved people and situations from my past. I try to avoid these thoughts because they lead to feelings of shame.

To dream about these folks and places was hard to shake off because I had no conscious mind involved in trying to stop the progression of my thoughts.

I woke up to a stomachache and thoughts like, "Man you've done some stupid things."

"Wow, you've spent alot of time drinking."

"How did you give your heart away to someone like that?"

"Nice job. You chose spending time with them over spending time with your daughter. You're not a very good mom."

"You're not a very good person."

"God can't really love you like you think He can."

"You simply aren't that loveable."

It took about a minute to spiral down into a pit of darkness. I was overwhelmed with feelings of shame, loneliness, sadness. Complete and utter defeat. I wanted to pull the covers over my head and sink into the nothingness I was certain I deserved.

Thankfully, I finally realized that I had a choice to live in this nasty place of rehashing sin and mistakes *or* I had a choice to turn to God and see myself as He sees me.

I had a choice to stay in darkness *or* I had a choice to move into the Light.

I had a choice to listen to me *or* to listen to God. I chose God.

Paul tells us in 2 Corinthians to *"take every thought captive"*! That's a powerful statement, don't you think?

Take your thoughts captive! This means when your thoughts are negative and draw you away from God, you should grab them by their scrawny little arms and say *"No."*

No, I will not think on you. *No*, I will not let you drag me into darkness. *No*, I will not let you move me away from my God.

Reliant

Instead, you run to the Lord crying out for new thoughts to replace them. Thoughts like these: I am a new creation in Christ (2 Corinthians 5:17); God loves me (John 3:16); I have God's grace (2 Corinthians 12:9); I am more than a conquerer in Christ (Romans 8:37); I have been given a spirit of power, love and self-discipline (2 Timothy 1:7).

We can't simply remove a thought. We have to replace it.

In order for me to stop thinking something, I have to start thinking about something else. When my thoughts start to go down the negative road I'm going to stop, turn around and start replacing those thoughts with scripture. God's Word is amazing!

God's Word has every answer we need and every response to go to war against those hurtful thoughts.

There is no value in beating ourselves up about the past sin in our lives … God doesn't do this! And, if God doesn't do it, we shouldn't either. 1 John 1:9 says if we confess our sins to God, He will not only forgive us but He'll go one step further and cleanse us!

Being clean means whatever condemnation was left from my sin is gone. I stand in front of God as a clean, forgiven child of His. I have no reason to start thinking about the dirt that was once on me unless I'm praising Him for removing it or sharing my story to help someone else.

God loves you so much and His entire Word is the story of that love. Don't waste one extra second thinking on things that move you away from that love. If you've confessed your sin and repented, then let it go. Give your negative thoughts to God. Ask Him to show you scripture to strengthen your spirit and your relationship with Him. God wants to live with you in every moment of your life so think on Him.

Journal Space

Living together

> *"So then you are no longer strangers and aliens, but you are fellow citizens with the saints and members of the household of God, built on the foundation of the apostles and prophets, Christ Jesus himself being the cornerstone, in whom the whole structure, being joined together, grows into a holy temple in the Lord."*
> Ephesians 2:19-21

Members of a household know each other's bad habits and good habits, know each other's quirks and mannerisms, know each other's burdens and joys. God has called us to be members of His household and yet we have a fear that if other people really knew us, they would reject us.

We have to remember our position before Christ. The wages of all sin is death (Romans 6:23), which means whatever sin you were delivered from is no worse and no better than the sin I was delivered from. All of us were headed to death before Christ saved us.

If we have been saved by grace (Ephesians 2:5), having had nothing to do with that salvation except have faith (Ephesians 2:8), then we have much in common. We all need grace and deserve death for our sins.

Reliant

We are offered salvation through Jesus. We all approach Jesus from the same place of need. And, without His free gift of salvation, we would never change. We would never grow. We would never be saved.

I shouldn't be ashamed of telling my story, the story of how I accepted God's gift of salvation once upon a time. And, I should also be able to talk about how I accept this gift of salvation every single day! I should be able to share my struggles, my challenges, the times when I want a drink, the times when I want a cigarette, the times when I laugh at something I really shouldn't and the times when I say something about someone that really wasn't very nice. For me, all of these things are habits from my life before Christ. Without repentance, they will keep me from being close to Him if I let them be a part of my daily experience.

I should be able to share these things about my journey with people without fear that they are going to reject me and they should be able to do the same with me. Jesus told us to come to Him when we are weary and carrying a heavy burden. In Him we will find rest (Matthew 11:28). If we are in Him, if the Holy Spirit lives in us, then we should also be able to come to each other and unload our burdens together.

My natural inclination is to retreat inward when I have a struggle, to withdraw from relationships. I do this because I know everyone else is dealing with their own struggles and I don't want to add any more weight. Truth be told, I don't always feel worthy of the extra support. However, that kind of thinking keeps me looking down at myself, instead of looking up toward God. If we are truly a household of believers, then we need to share our struggles and challenges — not to find a solution, but to find God.

As a community and a family, we need to be praying together, sharing our burdens and sharing our joys and praises. Members of the same household have no other choice because they are close together.

When I found myself at my lowest point in life, I found myself the most alone I've ever been. At any point during my downward spiral, I could have reached out to someone for help. If I had done that, I could have stopped myself before I reached such a low point. Instead, I kept my pain to myself.

I built walls and kept people at arm's length. I put on a smiley face when necessary, and said it was all OK, even when I didn't feel OK inside. I don't want to ever get to that point again. Even more, I don't want anyone who knows me to get to that point themselves.

I want to be a participant in the lives of the members of the household of God. I want to share the journey with my brothers and sisters in Christ, not just sit on the sidelines. I want to live life with them. I want us to be able to pray for and praise God with each other in detailed ways, not just general ones. And if you have a need that I can meet, I want to know about it so I can fill it. Keeping our needs to ourselves only keeps us in a needy place, and that's not what God intended.

Journal Space

Acting instead of reacting

"Then Simon Peter drew a sword and slashed off the right ear of Malchus, the high priest's slave." John 18:10 NLT

"Peter exclaimed, 'Rabbi, it's wonderful for us to be here! Let's make three shelters as memorials — one for you, one for Moses and one for Elijah.'" Mark 9:5 NLT

"So Peter went over the side of the boat and walked on the water toward Jesus. But when he saw the strong wind and the waves, he was terrified and began to sinkl 'Save me, Lord!' he shouted." Matthew 14:29b-30 NLT

While he was a new follower of Jesus, Peter was all heart, little head and completely committed to the moment, without thinking about what's next. Peter was focused on the here and now. He was about reacting, instead of acting. This allowed for some mountain-top experiences, like walking on water. It also allowed for some dark valley moments, like denying his involvement with Jesus.

I love Peter! I identify with Peter more than any other person written about in scripture. I have a huge desire to do a lot of things. My reaction to any given situation sometimes leads to me lopping off body parts (figuratively, of course), and sometimes leads to me screaming, "Save me, Lord!" because I get terrified.

Praise be to God that He loves me. And even better … that He is in the process of transforming me. Less pendulum swings … more centered on Jesus. Less reaction … more action. Less me … more Him.

God has put me in several situations where if I had acted the way my instinct and emotions guided, I would be in a constant state of apologizing for rash behavior which could have been avoided.

Don't get me wrong, I have no problem saying I did something wrong and then, seeking forgiveness. What I don't like is having to do it when the apology is the outcome of an outburst of emotion and reaction.

God is showing me that sometimes reacting rashly causes damage to relationships that can't be fixed. The damage can be repaired, but there is always a scar. I don't want to scar anyone, I want to love people. I want to be calm and thoughtful in challenging situations.

Thankfully God is right there in those times, taking my hand and guiding me. I can see Jesus' face in my mind. It's amazingly loving, yet his eyes pierce and see right through to my heart. He has a slight smile that says, "Trust me." His strong hand wraps around mine altogether saying, "I've got you. Don't look down. Don't get terrified. I've got you. Keep going." And through that love, I have the strength to keep growing, to go deeper and act more intentionally, instead react emotionally. Thank you, Jesus!

Growth is sometimes uncomfortable and painful. Growing pains don't stop just because we've gotten as tall as our physical bodies are going to get, they keep going as long as our spirit is here in order to make us the person we are meant to be. The joy in the pain and discomfort is that it's a sign that we are growing! Praise God when you feel the pain or ache! Praise Him that He's moving in your life and giving you opportunity to trust Him more.

Journal Space

Earnestly seeking

> *"And without faith it is impossible to please God, because anyone who comes to him must believe that he exists and that he rewards those who earnestly seek him." Hebrews 11:6 NIV*

Do you know what happens when you earnestly seek God? You receive peace! My life now has a measure of peace that it has never had before, and I can say that without exaggerating. Not too long ago, I was miserable most of the time. That, also, isn't an exaggeration.

I was drowning in a huge ocean of grief, anger and depression. I had compartmentalized my life to such a state that my closest friends and family didn't even know I was struggling. I was spending my free time with the wrong people, in the wrong places, doing the wrong things, and I was drowning. The scary part of all of it is that I was still functional. I was at work every day. I was at church every Sunday. I was at family gatherings every time we got together. I had completely compartmentalized my life.

God was the last person I was seeking. I was in church every Sunday and without fail, I would end in tears crying out for God to rescue me. Through my tears, He would lovingly say, "Give me your life."

Unfortunately, I was unwilling to give Him my life, to earnestly seek him. I was more interested in the pain and feeling cheated. I wanted the easy way out, and I knew God wanted the hard work. I wanted Him to rescue me and He wanted to transform me. I wanted freedom from the pain, but I didn't want the healing process.

Pain is a symptom and it reveals a problem which has to be fixed. My pain was over the sudden death of my mom who was honestly the glue that held my life together. That pain turned into anger and caused me to not pay attention to the kind of people I was allowing to influence my life. Those influences were leading me further and further away from God.

There's a verse in 1 Corinthians 15:33 which says, *"Do not be misled: 'Bad company corrupts good character.'" (NIV)* I fully believe that bad company is waiting on every corner. Bad company is attractive. It looks like something good, but it is deceptive and eventually fatal. Bad company may not kill your flesh right away, but it will kill your soul and your peace. It keeps you from faith and it keeps you from earnestly seeking God.

I felt that God had no place in my life because my perception of God was that He was mean and hurtful. I desperately longed to feel close to Him but for a time was completely unwilling to do what He was asking me to do, which was to give Him my life. Giving God my life, earnestly seeking Him, meant giving up people and things I thought I loved. Earnestly seeking God meant that I would have to trust that He really did love me and that He really was going to rescue me. Earnestly seeking Him meant that I would have to let him tear down all the walls, or compartments, I had built. But, I was terrified.

Kellyann Bowman

Activating my faith and earnestly seeking God has been a challenging and sometimes painful process, but the result has been my freedom. I am free to love God. I am free to love people. I am free to live the life God created me to live. I am free to not have compartments, or walls, in my life. I am free to be a member of my family in a way I never was before. I am free to be a better parent.

Journal Space

Love's recordkeeping

"[Love] keeps no record of wrongs." I Corinthians 13:5b NIV

I have a forgive-and-forget heart for everyone but myself. When it comes to myself and my actions, I have a great memory for the things I've done that I wish I hadn't done. I even rehearse them in my head. It's sometimes easy to forgive someone else, yet incredibly hard to forgive ourselves.

However, I am convinced that the longer we hold on to shame and regret, the longer we are living in slavery and bondage to the past and the further away we move from closeness with God. Here are a few verses that I believe we need to apply to ourselves and forgive ourselves in order to give us the freedom to love others and love God.

"The second [commandment] is this: 'Love your neighbor as yourself.' There is no commandment greater than these." Jesus, speaking in Mark 12:31 NIV

"There is no fear in love. But perfect love drives out fear, because fear has to do with punishment. The one who fears is not made perfect in love." 1 John 4:18 NIV

> *"[Love] always protects, always trusts, always hopes, always perseveres." 1 Corinthians 13:7 NIV*

When we read them at first, we believe them to be telling us how to love others. While this is true, it is also true that they are showing us how to love ourselves. When Jesus told us to love others the same way we love ourselves, doesn't it imply there is a level of self-love going on? Not arrogant, boastful or mean love, but rather, protecting, trusting, hoping, persevering love.

God's love is unconditional. No matter what you've done in your past, what you're doing in your present or what you'll do in your future, God's love is unending, steadfast and unconditional.

Your actions — both good and bad — have no impact on God's love for you. He's provided forgiveness before you even need it. Do you feel that? Do you grasp that? Your past, present and future actions, good and bad, don't draw God toward you or repel God away from you. (Say this out loud, "My past, present and future actions — both good and bad — don't draw or repel God.")

Here's what does happen though. Your past, present and future actions, good and bad, move you into closer relationship with or distance you from God. When you don't love yourself, when you don't forgive yourself, when you beat yourself up, you cause yourself to be further away from God. If love keeps no record of wrongs, then loving yourself means not keeping an internal record of wrongs. God has taken our sins, our mistakes, our regrets and thrown them as far as the *"east is from the west."* (Psalm 103:12)

God knows everything about us, and He loves us. God knows how we are formed (Psalm 103:14) and that we sin. Yet, He sent His Son to die for us in the midst of our sin (Romans 5:8). My heart's cry is for you to draw close to God. In order to do that fully, you must let go of your shame.

Give your wrongs to God, and let Him throw them as far as the east is from the west. Seek forgiveness for those things you haven't yet, make the changes you know He wants you to make in your life. Then, experience His peace and love for you in a new way — not through a filter of shame and regret over past actions.

God loves us so much and He wants to be close to us and so we need to let go. You can't change your past. All you can do is change your present and your future. I don't know about you, but I want all the freedom, forgiveness and love God wants to pour out on my life!

Journal Space

Refuge

> *"Then I pray to you, O Lord. I say, 'You are my place of refuge. You are all I really want in life.'" Psalm 142:5 NLT*

It is not always easy for me to be a single woman and think of God as my refuge. I want someone here and now to physically touch my arm, give me a hug and tell me it will be alright. I am a leader at work, at church and at home. I don't do those things because I seek attention, but because it is who God has made me. For the most part, I love it!

Yet, some days, I want to be the slacker who lives in her mom's basement playing video games all day covered in potato chip crumbs. I want everyone else to be accountable on their own. I don't want to hear the news of close friends being laid off, of people worrying about being fired, of my daughter complaining that I was being too hard on her for not doing her homework.

I woke up one morning and started crying immediately. Have you ever had a day like that? Where, when you wake up, you just feel off? I was letting the stress of this life get to me, and I was losing my eternal perspective. As soon as that happens, I start to feel overwhelmed.

I was facing a challenging conversation at work, following challenging conversations at home. I was trying to hold people accountable for their actions, when really all I wanted to do was say, "It's ok, I'll pick up your slack. Don't worry." I wanted someone to come in on a white horse, pick me up and carry me away. I wanted a place of refuge. I wanted it here on this earth, instead of knowing it is with my Redeemer Jesus and my heavenly Father.

Once I stepped out of my pity party and turned to my Refuge, everything changed. My day started in tears and ended with my daughter and I reading our favorite childhood books to each other. Through quiet time with God and quiet time with my daughter, God provided Himself as my refuge. God reached down, touched my arm and said, "It's going to be alright." As we prayed together and then chatted, I was struck with how amazing my life is and how all I really want is to be with God.

God is my husband. He is the one on the white horse who rides into my life to pick me up. The best part of that truth is He never rides out! On this day I forgot that I always have a place on God's "white horse." I thought I was alone on my own. Isaiah 54:5 says, *"For your Maker is your husband, the Lord of hosts is His name; and the Holy One of Israel is your Redeemer, the God of the whole earth He is called."* And then in verse 10 it says, *"'For the mountains may depart and the hills be removed, but my steadfast love shall not depart from you, and my covenant of peace shall not be removed,' says the Lord, who has compassion on you."*

Journal Space

Going fishing

"And He said to them, "Follow me, and I will make you fishers of men." Matthew 4:19

Jesus calls us to be "fishers of men." When I think about that, I feel instantly irritated because fishing is one of my least favorite things to do. If you ask me, fishing is boring, maybe the most boring thing anyone could do. You bait your hook, drop it in the water. Then, you wait for what feels like an eternity, hoping a fish will bite. Generally after trying in one area, you move to another spot and repeat the process of waiting. Sometimes, you get a bite on your line and get excited, but then the fish wiggles its way off the hook. Many times, you spend the entire day repeating the same process over and over only to return home with no fish.

Now I ask you, does that sound like fun? I know it does to some of you, but to me, it sounds like an exercise in futility.

However, now and then, when the timing is just right, you actually hook and reel in a fish. The joy and excitement makes you feel as if you might burst! You made it! You reached the finish line of the day's race … a fish in your possession! You take pictures of the fish. You have others take pictures of you holding the fish. You may even kiss the fish. Whichever route you to take to celebration, the goal has been accomplished.

Fishing, like ministry, takes time and patience, and I'm low on both. I shy away from those ministry opportunities that involve recruiting folks for my team. It feels the same as fishing. In fact, I don't really shy away, I absolutely avoid! I don't like reaching out to people over and over again, asking them for help, only to have them ignore me or even agree at first and cancel later.

I think of the time spent asking for volunteers as time spent dropping my line in the water. The people who never reply are like the fish swimming around my bait. The people who say yes and cancel are the other fish, the ones that get hooked and eventually wiggle off before I can get a commitment from them.

But every now and then, when the timing is right, someone says yes and follows through!

I have been part of a ministry team I love for a couple years now. Really, I only love about 90% of the position, though, because there is an element of "fishing" involved. As I've explained, I run away from these kinds of positions. I've actually considered stepping down from this role altogether because I dislike recruiting so much. I have a good friend who confronted me about this today and got me thinking about my actions. He said he sees impact potential in me that won't be used fully unless I get over this issue. I can't expect God to use me if I am unwilling to do what He has already called me to do … be a fisher of men.

On my own, I will never be a fisherman. Not even on my best day can I accomplish this task.

However, Jesus didn't say, "Go out on your own. Fish, and see what happens." Instead, Jesus said, "Follow me, and I will make you fishers of men." This translates to my life: *Kellyann, stop running from my will, and just follow me, and I will do the work through you. Then, you will be a fisher of men.* I have to stay persistent, keep asking people to serve with this goal in mind, and then, celebrate when they do.

Journal Space

Insurmountable

> *"And when those who carried the ark came into the Jordan, and the feet of the priests carrying the ark were dipped in the edge of the water (for the Jordan overflows all its banks all the days of harvest), the waters which were flowing down from above stood and rose up in one heap, a great distance away at Adam, the city that is beside Zarethan; and those which were flowing down toward the sea of the Arabah, the Salt Sea, were completely cut off. So the people crossed opposite Jericho. And the priests who carried the ark of the covenant of the Lord stood firm on dry ground in the middle of the Jordan while all Israel crossed on dry ground, until all the nation had finished crossing the Jordan." Joshua 3:15-17 NASB*

When the stakes are low, trust is naturally high. But, our God — the God of Adam, Abraham, Noah, Esther, Moses, Joshua, Rahab and David — is not a God of low stakes.

I'm not saying that God will only call us to tasks with high stakes. I am saying that God is not bound to consider the stakes at all. He just calls. It was no surprise to Him that the Israelites had to cross the Jordan at a time when the river was at its highest, but I'm willing to bet it was a surprise to them. Can't you just hear the crowds asking each other how on earth they were going to get across the raging river? Don't you think some of them thought Joshua must be crazy?

I'm certain the last person in line thought they had the best place, because they would see what was going to happen first and be able to make another plan. Of course, the Bible doesn't tell us any of that, so it's just my imagination playing with the words, but I'm sure some of the Israelites were wondering how God was going to help them face this seemingly insurmountable task.

As God often does, He provides in a big way! He creates a holy dam with a wall of water and they just walk through on dry ground. Who saw that coming? I doubt any of the Israelites did. The insurmountable became the conquered. And, once again, God shows He's got a plan — and the power to see the plan to fruition.

Insurmountable means the task at hand is just too great to overcome. How many times do we feel God moving us in a direction and our first reaction is, "No way! I can't do that! I'm not equipped to talk to those people! I can't move my family there!"

There are countless examples of "No" answers we give because we feel the thing God is asking us to do is insurmountable. And in the end, it's an issue of trust, because it's not so much that we think we *can't* do something, it's that we don't believe God *can*.

It's easy to follow God when it's easy, right? I can trust God to get me to church on Sunday, help me have a challenging conversation or help me rearrange my schedule to have more quiet time with him. But can I trust Him with my family, my fears and my finances?

We have to stop trying to figure out a human answer to God's superhuman call and just listen for His instruction. He didn't lead the Israelites to the river and then say, "OK, Kids. Today's challenge is how to get thousands of people across a raging river!" He didn't tell them to do it their own way.

He simply told Joshua to lead the priests to take a step in the river and wait for God to show His answer. The insurmountable is always surmountable when it is God's call on your life. Don't focus on the circumstance and get frightened. Step into the circumstance and see what God will do. There's no question that if He's calling you to do something, then He's there with you, and He's already got the path laid out.

Step into the river, step into the circumstance. Trust.

Journal Space